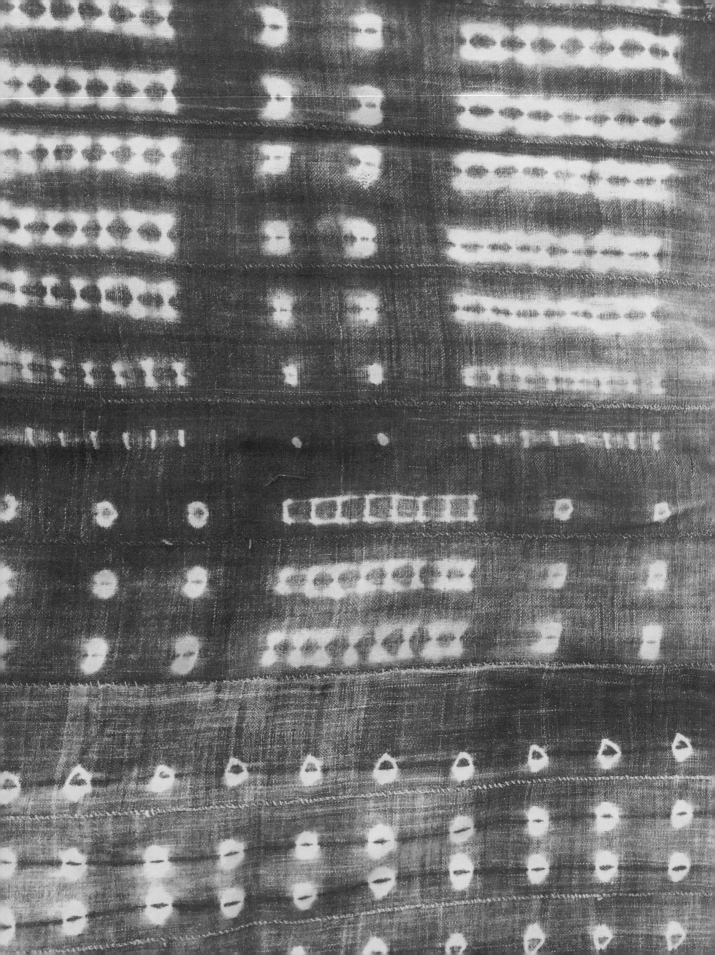

Our clan from left to right:
Angus Finley Corbin Digby Henry Amanda Oliver

OPEN HOUSE

OPEN HOUSE
Reinventing Space for Simple Living

Amanda Pays & Corbin Bernsen

GIBBS SMITH
TO ENRICH AND INSPIRE HUMANKIND

CONTENTS

PREFACE

by Corbin Bernsen

When I hit the scene with the sudden explosion of "LA Law," it essentially put me on the "map," and to be very frank, I quickly adopted the blind notion that I was the "Be All and End All." I was easily fooled into thinking that all things related to me—my thoughts and ideas specifically, having come from me, had an irrevocable place and order that was final. The result of that brilliant outlook: unhappiness. Despite an outward trajectory that was skyrocketing, there was an emptiness, and dare I say, a dark pall over what should have been days filled with light.

Before all that, however, I put myself through college as a carpenter. I framed houses. I loved to swing a hammer and build things, though more often than not I found myself digging trenches for the foundations of the houses. Not bad, learning about and appreciating foundations and their metaphorical extension. It was and remains an invaluable education.

So years later, when I was able to purchase my first house from the riches of my newly minted "Hollywood success," it was no surprise to friends and family that I would immediately proceed to deconstruct the basic Laurel Canyon home that I'd purchased and turn it into something special. The style of the day was Santa Fe. Given my Cherokee roots and a general leaning toward spirituality, it was a match made in heaven, so to speak. Three months and several thousand dollars later, I had transformed my basic dwelling into what I thought was a New Mexican masterpiece! It had round beams, salvaged doors from Mexico, Saltillo tiles, and my first art purchase—a John Nieto painting of a colorful Indian chief to hang over the fireplace. Perfection! The disorder of my life, created in part by my new success, I suddenly found back in order—or so I thought. Then I met Amanda. Having her own deep roots in design and renovation, courtesy of an incredible father who not only was handy but genuinely enjoyed moving and "fixing up" homes—if even as a survival mechanism—she developed an early skill and remarkable eye for the necessary components of what it takes to make over a room or house.

I met Amanda in a nightclub (very Hollywood) and declared to a friend the following day with great excitement and commitment, "I'm going to marry that girl!" And why not? I had a career, a Corvette, a few bucks in the bank, and my newly self- renovated Santa Fe casa in the hills. What girl could ask for more? Well . . . Amanda! The full story has more hours and days than suggested here, but the short version is that she walked into my masterpiece of a home, took one look at it and said, "All this has to go!" Talk about a potential deal breaker and the ultimate ego killer! But I had this other thing going on—this committed vision of a life with Amanda that I had shared with my friend. Destiny was not to be denied! So I had to make the first truly big choice of my new success as the "it" guy in town: tell Amanda Pays—also on her own trajectory in town—to take a hike or . . . God forbid . . . yield! Was I willing to knock down the walls behind my gut reaction and impulsive resistance to allow another view in? Was I willing to create a window to my soul that might allow new light? And here's the funny thing: beyond some of the "design stuff," it was also exactly what she was suggesting I do with my home! Open up walls, create windows, allow in new light and experience a view of the hills that I had simply neglected to see. And so it began, a shared adventure in the designs of our homes and our life together.

Amanda and I have been married for nearly thirty years now, and over the course of our marriage—half our lives—the question we are asked most is "What is the key to a successful marriage?" Several answers have come up, from the obvious "We're best friends" and "We share common interests" to the longer view of having built a solid foundation of trust and a strong bond. Or even a deeper knowledge that we simply complement one another, yin and yang and all that.

In recent years, however, I've come to a richer understanding of our "oneness," a notion I suppose has been strengthened by the simple arithmetic of our years together, not to mention the numerous homes that we've renovated together, and for the most part, actually lived in. The reality is that, fundamentally, beginning with those Laurel Canyon days, we have become two people who genuinely aren't afraid to knock down walls and barriers, and allow new thought and ideas—new light—to permeate our lives. And perhaps even more importantly, we understand and embrace the fear, doubt and concerns that might come with that type of commitment, knowing that somewhere behind those walls, with the benefit of illumination, great treasures are waiting!

It's no wonder, then, that what has developed as a common passion — the reinventing and the reimagining of numerous homes for our family to live in — is a direct reflection of who we are as a couple. I believe that is the key to our marriage, a bond created by a common willingness to tear down walls and allow light to expose our love. Our minds and our hearts are an Open House.

OUR STORY

by Amanda Pays

Corbin actually tells the story as it was—and not long after that first "sighting" in the nightclub, we were in a red Corvette on our way to a candlelit dinner. I guess you could say we fell in love really, really fast, because within weeks we were living together in his Laurel Canyon pad! Looking back, he had some really beautiful pieces that I made him sell, but we agreed to redecorate in a style incorporating the various flourishes we could appreciate in each other and discovered some happy compromises along the way.

Corbin was already shopping at Arte de Mexico, a furnishings emporium that specialized in artisanal goods from South of the Border and a shop I loved as well, and I was able to mix in my own clean, crisp, unfussy English style. Together we started going to area flea markets, where we discovered we both shared an enduring penchant for authentic materials: the hard-worn patina of discarded salvage and junk, abandoned and orphaned architectural elements, the heartwarming burnish of reclaimed woods. Beautiful materials proved to be something of an aphrodisiac for us and a signature that has stood the test of time.

In the end our redesign of Corbin's southwestern home became a harmonious fusion of Rustic Americana and stripped-down English Country. I don't know what to call that or anything we've done since, but it is a look that is unique to us and has proved to be both comfortable and aesthetically successful.

Materials
_____
Beverly Hills

It was a year after Corbin and I met, we were married and expecting our first son, that we set out to find our first home as newlyweds about to start a family, albeit with a Hollywood budget and an English exile's laundry list of prerequisites and deal killers. After a quick search, we found ourselves completely besotted with a 1,500-square-foot fixer-upper tucked off a picturesque canyon rising above Sunset Boulevard in the heart of Beverly Hills. This little charmer sat on its own knoll at the end of a cul de sac.

Even though we had set out to split the difference between our two tastes, this property was the closest I'd seen to anything resembling a truly authentic English cottage. In fact, the back garden was so evocative of England that I could forget the coyote-crowded barranca just beyond the trained roses out back. My heart actually skipped a beat, and Corbin was right there with me.

What it would ultimately look like was anyone's guess, but the two of us were convinced that whatever ensued from our collaboration would look amazing! Against the advice of our business manager, we bought it. The number cruncher was no match for the powerful persuasion of the half-acre lot with a Cotswoldian vibe. Besides, we were two gainfully employed actors on hit TV shows—was there any unforeseen consequence we couldn't negotiate with a robust checkbook?

The original house already suggested the architectural idiom we both wanted—a half-timbered Tudor type with the informality of a farmhouse. We turned to an architect to collaborate on a sprawling design expansion that would incorporate all the styles of all the places we had loved all at once and in one place.

More, more, more, and right now!

Vintage pine interior doors were part of our shipment from Drummonds of Bramley in the UK.

"No expense spared" was an under-statement on this house. For example, while on a job together, Judd Hirsch told Corbin about his soon-to-be-demolished old barn back East and the quality of the interior support beams. His description was so compelling and our own aesthetic weakness for reclaimed old-growth wood so great, that right there on the spot Corbin agreed to dismantle and ship the entire barn for re-use. And thus our recycling journey began!

Once we broke ground, the project moved forward slowly, what with the scope and complexity of our dreams; and like sand through an hourglass, the money drained. Actually, the money drained much faster than the project crawled, but we were in with both feet at this point. Every so often, Corbin and I would try to think of ways to cut corners and shave time and dollars off of our runaway train, but we were so far along the tracks that it would have been more costly to scale back and force even more design revisions. So we just plowed ahead with the building of our 9500 sq ft dream house.

Corbin did, however, successfully suggest to the guy with the front-end loading tractor to stop giving our then two-year-old son, Oliver, earth-moving instruction and start actually moving the earth—so that was a step forward!

But then there were steps back—like the incorporation and installation of each new "old" find—that would create a distinct challenge for our contractor, a lifelong friend who'd actually taught Corbin almost everything about carpentry as a teenager.

Corbin and I both got carried away with our fascination for great authentic materials, like the meandering stone walls and terraces throughout Europe. So much so, that we managed to outstrip the California quarry supply with the amount of stone walls and patios we added to our landscape design.

We went all out on the custom-made limestone fireplace and Bennison-upholstered George Smith sofas and chairs. We were having fun!

But perhaps the ultimate indulgence on this Beverly Hills house was the tunnel. One day while overseeing the framing of the recreation room in one of the far-flung wings of the house, Corbin came to the realization that it was going to be a long tramp around the U-shaped house to get from his playroom to the kitchen for dinner, a snack, a beer, or whatever.

And then it happened: inspiration. Corbin looked meaningfully across the garden and noticed the kitchen "just over there." After a quick discussion with our contractor and agreeing on a price, Corbin said "Dig," and off they went to dig a tunnel! I was more than a willing accomplice in this folly of follies, demanding that the indispensable tunnel be as remarkable and authentic as the rest of the house—a coved ceiling, plastered walls, and a path of creamy limestone pavers.

It was not cheap or even haphazardly economical, but how do you hold back when you've already embarked on the construction of a tunnel in a private residence in Beverly Hills?

Our shipment from the UK also included this clawfoot tub, faucets and heated towel rail (originally out of the Dorchester Hotel) via Drummonds of Bramley.

This stripe from Ralph Lauren Home Collection gives the bathroom a fresh, clean feel.

Yes, we knew it was crazy to go on such an international bender when great material was available much closer to home, but this was to be our dream house, the place to raise a family, where our life would happen within close striking distance of our careers.

Amortized over twenty something years, even the expense of the tunnel became reasonable. And we did find a lot of things locally, at the Rose Bowl flea market, even our bed at LA's Arte de Mexico.

Three years and two babies later, we were finally able to move in, and with the help of an outstanding Irish couple and a divine Welsh nanny, we had everything we could ever wish for.

But the forces at large conspired against us. Within a year, we found ourselves plummeting back down to earth from our heady perch. The Northridge quake in '94 shook our family to the core, followed by the aftershock of the cancellation of Corbin's long-running show. There was damage to the house, staff to be paid, and I had now decided to become a full-time mother—coupled with second thoughts about living in Los Angeles, away from the glitz and glamour of Hollywood and perhaps wanting our children to experience the country where I had grown up and get a taste of my roots in English countryside. So when actor Steve Martin showed up at the house one day to have a look at what we had done and said "Can I have it all?" we answered "Yes." And that was that.

MATERIAL STATEMENTS

The teak floors were sourced from Bali.

We imported handmade tiles from Mexico to give the house a rustic feel.

We left the interior walls unpainted for a luminous matte effect.

Sigfrid, our eccentric iron monger, custom made all railings.

We faced all exterior walls with California sandstone.

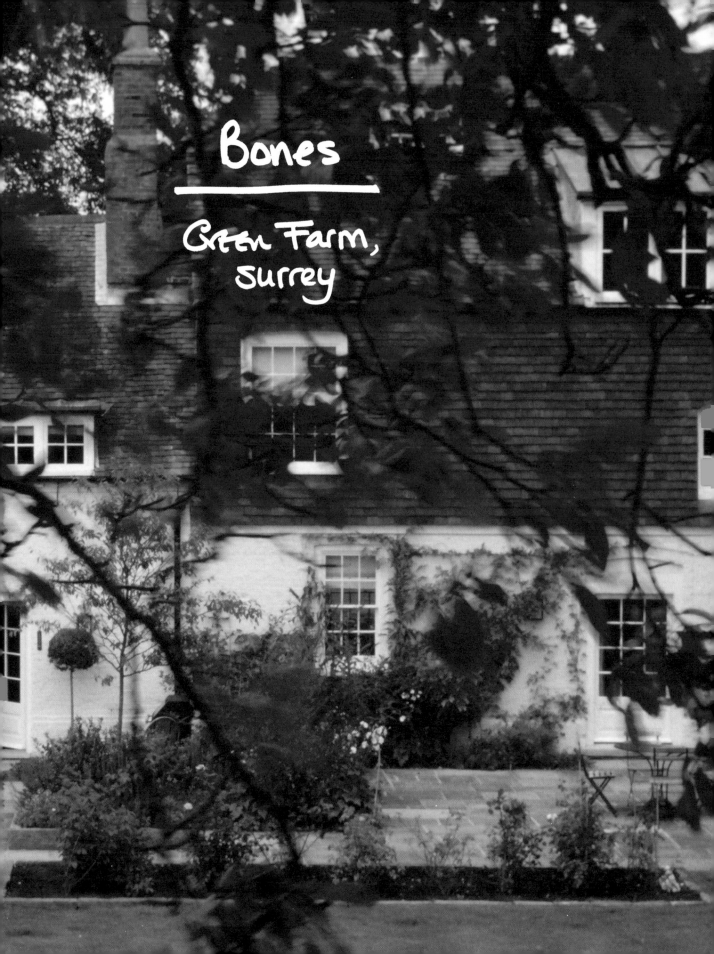

Bones
_____

Green Farm,
Surrey

So we all moved to England and camped out in my father's guest cottage while Corbin and I searched for the venue of our next phase. Corbin was an incredibly good sport with this impetuous move halfway around the world and into the very bosom of his wife's eccentric extended family. Then there were the idiosyncrasies of life in rural England—pubs, port, cigars, waistcoats and bangers! Despite the grandeur of our previous collaboration, we now knew we made an excellent team and would have a great time taking on anything new and challenging.

Lessons from the Beverly Hills extravaganza learned, we agreed to scale back. Way back. We wanted sensible comfort—nothing more—and I already had an image of the perfect home for our family and newfound simplicity: a standard-issue brick Georgian house in the rolling countryside of Surrey, close to my dear father and not prohibitively far from friends and resources in London and the professionally necessary Heathrow.

For a year we crisscrossed the country lanes with a son or two riding alongside. I felt resourceful and frugal at the same time in my eight-seater used, old-school Land Rover. The impromptu homecoming, the beach boy husband, the co-pilot twins, the prodigal daughter that was me, the rainy landscape, and the no-frills wheels eventually drew us all to a picture-perfect house on an impossibly picturesque thirty acres of green pasture.

Green Farm was exactly what I'd set out to find. I loved it at first sight and at last glance. Because what it had—despite the cracked floors, peeling walls and sagging ceilings—was great bones!

Georgian style is extremely straightforward, and Green Farm delivered on all scores. The front door opened onto a hallway with rooms symmetrically lined up on either side. Other major features included interior plastering and oak paneling, oak staircase and banister executions, and sash windows and brick walling outside. No need to paint the grass green in Surrey, or mask concrete block walls with a veneer of fieldstone. It was already there.

Corbin and I agreed to retain and preserve as much as possible of everything we found in situ at Green Farm. This was the original fundamental shift in the design modus operandi we would hone over the ensuing decades. Obviously, it was much easier to perfect a room's aesthetics after a down-to-the-studs demo, but who would feel so entitled to rip apart Green Farm's extraordinary bones? Or be so ruthless?

One upgrade that needed no discussion—the plumbing!

The bulk of the original structure dated to two very distinct periods: the virtually medieval 1400s and the post-Renaissance 1700s. How different from our last remodel of a 1930s Los Angeles structure. At the onset of this renovation, we were humbled by the longevity of everything on the site and felt more like stewards of the property than rehabilitators.

We took the task of respectfully updating this piece of architectural history seriously, while highlighting and conserving the hallmark characteristics we were thankful to find when we arrived, like some of the fantastic eighteenth-century wall paneling and an original inglenook fireplace from the 1400s.

We were fortunate to find a brilliant construction firm within a few miles of the house that was familiar with the property and cognizant of any roadblocks that we might encounter, such as repairing interior walls that had been originally constructed with horsehair plaster. This firm had access to local craftsmen who eagerly custom built all the additional cabinetry, windows, doors, flooring and even the double-sized bunk beds Corbin designed for our growing family of boys.

Who would have thought that Corbin's Santa Fe bedframe was going to look so perfect in this house?

Virtually everything we used at Green Farm was hand-crafted on-site or within a dozen or so miles from where it would be installed. No more containers or shipping of stone. We refurbished as many windows and doors as possible, stripping decades of paint and glazer's putty and replacing panes of injured ancient glass with mint-condition fresh glass. Our local carpenter was incredibly diligent in this process and was able to replicate anything no longer in existence, from extra-deep windowsills to bowed banister frames.

To our surprise, we discovered and preserved some fifty slabs of original field-dressed limestone we found curiously buried in the garden. You already know how much we love legacy, so the decision to repurpose these slabs as flooring in our kitchen, laundry room and entrance hall was a no-brainer!

Room by room, this old Georgian pile came roaring back to life.

As far as furnishing the house went, I also sourced everything locally. The dining table and chairs came from an antiques shop just down the road in Farnham, and all my favorite designer brands—George Smith, Bennison, Farrow and Ball, Ian Mankin—were now only an hour away!

Mohair Velvet, reseda George Smith

Linen 25, Ivory Ian Mankin

Empire 1, Peony Ian Mankin

Cinnabar, faded on beige Bennison

Even our back patio came from the surrounds of London—stone pavements that were sitting idle and begging to be reused if the price was right, which it was. We actually had them cut up into three different sizes to add interest to the layout.

Ultimately, we turned this charming farm property into a comfortable family home: a lovely compilation of five bedrooms and four bathrooms, with a classic English study painted the delicious Farrow and Ball "Drawing Room Blue." And the uber-traditional boot/laundry room, which featured a luxurious import I forgot to mention—two commercial-size top-loading U.S.-manufactured washing machines (horrifyingly vulgar to all the locals, obviously); but this was Corbin's one and only capitulation to American convenience. Not exactly a tunnel to the kitchen, but we did have a lot of muddy boys in tow, so I was happy to bend the rules for him.

Oh, one other thing. I should probably mention that we rented the cottage next door to house Corbin's snow globe collection, 8,000 and counting!

We finally moved into this stunning new/old brick and mortar home and threw a spectacular Christmas party to celebrate our collaborative rehabilitation of a local treasure.

Corbin had even built a treehouse with the boys. And in a few months I gave birth to Finley—boy number four.

Corbin and I continued to juggle our busy professional lives, and we all learned to fully embrace the rain, the roaring fires and the local pub. It was indeed the antidote to what had become of us back in Beverly Hills, a dream I'd had thousands of miles away of what my life could be like. And it pretty much came through hard work and a lot of help from boots on the ground.

After three years or so, England became rather bleak to my Anglo-Californian sensibility. The lushness of the ever-present rain became anathema to our boys as their memories of their dad's favorite beach breaks became paler still. And I realized that we could not live for much longer without more sunshine. Whether it was one part post-partum depression on my end or three parts hearing my toddler sons groan and balk at the prospect of another soggy bag of crisps at the local pub, I had come to another of my epiphanies: we were going to need to, once again—head west. Stay tuned!

IN KEEPING WITH THE PERIOD

Another great refurbished tub we sourced, coupled with a beautiful pair of Czech & Speake faucets from London.

Our carpenter custom made all doors in keeping with the period.

Choosing the right green for our front door with Farrow and Ball's beautiful palette. This one is "Green Smoke."

Created in 1929, the Aga range has become the epitome of country kitchen style.

We were even able to use remnants of the limestone for this fireplace hearth.

HONING OUR CRAFT

Within a week of my eureka moment in sodden Surrey, we were back in LA, camped out in the venerable, funky Chateau Marmont Hotel on Sunset Boulevard at the foot of the Hollywood Hills. In retrospect, this was the beginning of a five-year period where we bounced around from house to house like a band of mad gypsies.

These were the good-old days, before all the present-day house-flipping mania. There were fewer players on the board and a lot of prime inventory for sale, most of it untouched since its original construction.

The conditions were ideal for Corbin and me to plunge into the market and really hone our craft renovation-wise. We became addicted to house hunting. We genuinely loved scanning the listings, driving around, seeing what was out there. We realized our rare knack was finding the elusive diamonds in the rough—those houses that other hunters weren't "getting"—and bringing new life and resale value to these ugly ducklings hiding in plain sight on the streets of LA.

By the time we were ready to settle down for a while, we'd had a blistering run of renovation, starting with a Cape Cod–style cottage in the Hollywood Hills and ending with a barn in Encino. At this point, we were really good at fixer-upping. What we didn't know was that we were actually building a real business!

Space
Studio City

Which brings us to this renovation project, the house that would become a true home for our family for any real length of time, the place where our boys grew into young men.

One day Corbin and I happened to drive by an "Open House" sign in nearby Studio City and impulsively pulled over to check it out. A crowd of looky-loos were already wandering around the property, which could only be semi-generously described as Tudoresque.

This 1940s brick number could not have been darker or more uncomfortably divided on the inside: nonsensical layout of rooms and arbitrary window and door placements to start. There was an architect's vision somewhere, but we couldn't see it.

The grounds were no better: wildly overgrown with meandering cacti and succulents, assorted ornamental shrubbery, masses of weeds and one beautiful fully grown orange tree in full fruit. An above-ground pool in disrepair and a decrepit work shed completed the scenery.

Every house hunter, ourselves included, could see this was a fixer-upper of Herculean proportions, but Corbin and I had by now developed an eye for seeing "size" and could easily imagine reassigning interior square footage and inverting bedrooms and bathrooms. This one would be infinitely more cost effective than the page-one rewrite we had started out with in Beverly Hills.

Every renovation is a judgment call based on your level of sophistication, expertise and tolerance for risk and gyp board dust. Some projects are not worth undertaking, but many others reveal themselves to be manageable and ultimately profitable if you can tease out those alterations that are smart and avoid those that are too risky.

Our first purchase for the house, was a massive pair of vintage steel-and-glass French doors and a pair of antique factory windows, which became the design springboard for the rest of the house.

Corbin and I knew instantly that we could open up the entire house and reassign wasted space and redundant hallways into an expanse of flowing rooms. We would add an enormous kitchen/dining space combo that would become the de facto nucleus of the house, a place where we and our guests would want to congregate. By creating an open floor plan, an inviting home would be apparent the minute you stepped through the front door.

The existing living room had been forced to serve as a passageway to a hall, two bedrooms and a tiny shared bathroom. So we decided to convert one bedroom into a cozy library/family room. We also added approximately 1,000 square feet that went upstairs and pushed out downstairs to create three bedrooms and bathrooms. The house was beginning to feel like a family home.

Similarly, the original layout required passing through the dining room to get to the kitchen, an awkward arrangement that dead-ended at the maid's room. Since we were going to build the "piece de resistance" of a kitchen/dining space, we were able to repurpose the original dining room into a media room, with walls lined in Oliver's dynamic, handmade wallpaper. He printed enlarged copies of his photography and collaged them onto the walls, then gray-washed them with a final seal coat of matte varnish.
Beautiful and unique!

Our quest to bring in more light wherever possible included replacing leaded glass windows with larger, single-pane ones, enlarging interior doorways and openings and installing chunky reclaimed whitewashed Brazilian wood headers. These big, beautiful beams added a stroke of rusticity to our increasingly less-formal design.

I painted the interior walls and ceilings a cool shade of white, almost grayish, that recalls a Nordic white of the Danes or the Dutch and which glows pearly smooth when hit with the California sun. I love how the color recedes and advances depending on the time of day. Remember, white is isn't the absence of color but the amalgamation of all colors. This shade coupled with the gray-washed floors have become components of what has evolved into our signature style.

| Plaster of Paris | Decorators white | Simply white | Stonington gray |

by Sydney Harbor   rest by Benjamin Moore

We stretched our budget again with regard to new flooring when we found an artisan who was great with blue flagstone and had had excellent results installing this traditionally outdoor material inside. We used it in all the bathrooms, the utility room and the office, and the effect was cool and sleek.

During the demo phase of the house, we uncovered three original steel-and-chicken wire glass skylights hidden behind opaque plastic coverings—a real eureka moment!

We decided to reuse these in our new kitchen and also integrated the chicken wire idea into the upper cabinets, windows and doors in this room. As you can see, a lot of what looks completely preplanned is really just a series of happy accidents, and in fact the best of all design options.

As the renovation progressed, we could feel this beautiful eclectic aesthetic revealing itself to us as we peeled away layers of the original house. For the cabinetry we recut more reclaimed Brazilian boards and fitted them with a bag of fifty vintage handles that we had snagged at a local swap meet. With a screed of fresh concrete on the floor, this kitchen was becoming a new hub for the house and was taking on a kind of industrial country feel, bright with lots of natural light.

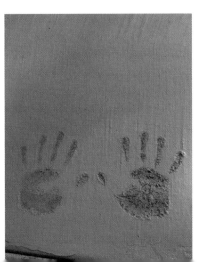

We created the opening for this antique steel bank door and put in opaque chicken wire glass in for privacy.

We believe in continuity of materials throughout a home—cabinetry, countertops, hardware, and flooring.

I used prewashed drop cloth material to make all of the window blinds.

We found this old tub and had it refurbished and custom painted to suit our palette.

As we had to tighten our budget belt, I pulled out all my creative stops, finding gray and flax linen from Ikea for $5 a yard to cover all of our flea market sofas and chairs.

The interior space was now coming together as we combined Moroccan Berber rugs, contemporary reclaimed coffee tables with eclectic lighting. Even the "old-timers," like the French marble-topped steel table, managed to find their place.

MAKING SPACE FOR THE BOYS

It's one thing to not waste space but an entirely different thing to exploit the space at hand. Our Studio City house came with a large work shed in the back garden. Corbin thought we could convert it into a bunkhouse for our three oldest boys. With no room for expansion, Corbin had to coax utility out of every square inch. And he's a genius at this.

He set to work by dividing the square footage into two bedrooms separated by a ladder to a mezzanine third bedroom carved out of original headroom.

Underneath the treads of the stairway, he created closets, open shelving and cubicles for each of the two ground-floor bedrooms. He insulated the place and lined it with reclaimed siding.

At Olde Good Things in downtown LA we found vintage nautical sconces for over-bed lighting and another pair of steel-and-glass doors. We made small bedside shelves out of the remaining pieces of scaffold planks we had saved from the home's new staircase. Corbin's forte is finding a place for everything! Nothing goes to waste.

This ad hoc bunkhouse became an unofficial club-house, and for years it was jammed to its white-washed rafters with rambunctious teenage boys! If you build it, they will come.

We whitewashed literally everything that wasn't metal or glass, which didn't technically save or recover any space but did make the room feel less claustrophobic.

I hung painters drop cloth curtains on narrow-gauge galvanized plumber's piping, which we also used for the handrail on Corbin's ladder.

The last stage of the renovation involved a total re-landscaping of the grounds and additional stonework around the pool.

We cleared the property of overgrown shrubbery and old cacti and were instantly rewarded with light and views that hadn't been there during the open house. To preserve this openness, we held back on introducing too many elements to the newly liberated grounds. I used a lot of decomposed granite (or DG, as we refer to it) for pathways and even as ground cover because it is long-lasting and hard-wearing and has become an essential component to a water-wise landscape scheme, not to mention its golden beauty. This coupled with the olive tress and purple lavenders lent an almost gauzy interest of sage green and grayish trunks to the grounds without being too heavy-handed and dominant.

Our talented stonemason was able to match the original stonework when adding these new steps to the pool.

We kept the planting to a minimum, just olive trees and lavender.

When the year-long renovation was finally completed and the six of us had moved in, we all realized that we had created a truly unique family home with a Tudor-industrial twist without going off the deep end with our budget. We had turned frugality into an overarching design economy that transcended itself to become our new aesthetic. This was the moment I came to understand that the turnover revenue we were achieving was not just the simple appreciation of the real estate market; it was also a reflection of our personal style.

As our boys started trudging off into the world and Corbin's work commitments became more demanding, I realized I wanted to remain busy and productive, so I decided to venture off and undertake a couple of speculative projects on my own.

RESTORE - REUSE - RECYCLE

We made shelving all around the house out of aged scaffold planks that we bought from our builder for $10 a plank.

I found this pair of unique wall sconces made from old bread tins at Big Daddy's Antiques.

We collected a bunch of similarly patinated vintage work stools that sat perfectly around our kitchen island.

On a trip to Marrakesh, we discovered these beautiful, chunky brass taps at the souk. They made their way into our powder room.

This is how we really saved some dollars: making curtain poles and hand rails out of galvanized plumber's piping.

Budget

Hollywood Hills

Once I realized that my itinerant house renovation was something like an actual job—a day job and not just some ad hoc *vocation en famille* that generated a revenue stream—I decided to treat our house flipping as a professional numbers-driven enterprise. One with an actual budget that would constrain my occasional flights of aesthetic whimsy. One with a formal timetable for completion. I thought, if the market is validating my sense of architectural design, interior decoration and garden installation, then I may as well go for it and be great at it.

Being "great" meant buying lackluster listings at the right price with a total renovation budget and time frame in mind, but still implementing the signature style that Corbin and I had already developed and then delivering the project to market with enough aesthetic panache to sell quickly for top dollar.

As luck would have it, right out of the gate I was shown a pocket listing by an agent I had been working with. The house was quietly being offered at a great price, given its "marquee" location in the desirable Hollywood Hills, a picturesque tangle of streets high above the Sunset Strip.

As soon as I arrived, I noticed the hilly grounds were spectacularly overgrown, and I immediately envisioned the amazing city views I could reveal and reframe. The allure of the view would be an amazing selling point I could use, but I also wondered why I was the only buyer looking at this "diamond in the rough"—and then I stepped inside. It was the definition of deferred maintenance—structurally, mechanically and cosmetically. Vast expanses of personal clutter were masking a diorama of odd taste.

I understood that to get any traction on the market I would need to build a brand-new master suite, adding expensive square footage; but the price was low enough, and I knew I could make it uniquely beautiful and that when I re-listed the burnished result, the market would agree with me.

My offer was quickly accepted and I was off and running!

In order to get a jump on things, my contractor and I hashed out a very real scheme to remove walls and expand openings to create the "hub" format that I'd grown to love. We figured out how all of this could be accomplished structurally without outlandish expense, and we further agreed that it would make an enormous impact on the flow and feel of the existing claustrophobic interior.

And then we tackled the missing master suite and where it could logistically be situated and what it would cost. We came up with a realistic, if not slightly tight, budget. This was going to test my "saving" abilities!

I immediately hired an excellent draftsman to create the blueprints for my design of the master suite, which was the first big save on our budget. If the new construction is limited in scope, then there's no need to splurge on an architect, and Corbin and I felt pretty confident that we had, by now, developed a keen eye for design while keeping the integrity of the properties' architectural history.

While we waited for the permits to come through, I went to town on clearing the grounds of any accumulated debris and any excess specimen trees that could be relocated or removed, together with opening up and reconfiguring of walls and rooms on the inside.

The removal of interior walls and liberating the dedicated corridors created a series of living spaces that flowed beautifully into one another. The melding of the kitchen with the dining room created one big arena. And by doubling the size of the windows wherever possible by adding sliding doors, I created an accessibility to the outdoors that was breathtaking. We're in California, people! We have magnificent vistas and endless sunshine!

Other more reflexive decisions were made but not at the expense of the budget. Replacing the heavy volcanic rock fireplace wall with a simple coat of smooth plaster while saving the cool stone slab hearth was a game changer. The original kitchen cabinetry, however, I couldn't get rid of fast enough and I replaced it with clean-lined black Ikea cabinets, in keeping with the midcentury modern feel of the house.

I also used my go-to favorite white subway tile for all the bathrooms and accented with a pale gray grout from the budget friendly Home Depot or Lowe's.

The floors turned out to be original oak in great condition, so I decided to carry this look into the new master to unify the old with the new, and I also used oak to fill in where room reassignment had left gaps. Fresh oak strip flooring was really inexpensive, and when the original floors and the new batch were both painted with my signature pickled gray stain, the effect was a seamless silvery sheen that caught the light beautifully and yet remained very tactile and a joy to walk across in bare feet.

I deviated from this blanched oak for the bathrooms and utility spaces with a warm neutral dove gray slate.

I'm still very proud of the way that I managed the scope and execution of this renovation. With the help of an excellent draftsman and a general contractor, I was able to avoid costly change orders and impulse extravagances that might have tripped me up in the past. I discovered that a little restraint put my creativity to work, and I often came up with better solutions to other types of problems that came up. On this project, I developed a way to stick to my budget's line items. I discovered how to negotiate—with myself. For example, I found sinks at Habitat for Humanity for ten bucks each, and bought ends of marble slabs from fabricators deep in the San Fernando Valley for next to nothing, which liberated extra funds for an emerging necessity: defining the exterior grounds with landscape fencing.

When the work was finally completed, I could not have been more pleased with the ravishing-looking house we had exhumed from the overgrown dump, even with a stringent budget.

Outside I was ruthless with clearing and removing old plantings. Corbin built new wooden fences that circumscribed the property, which we painted a pale shade of gray-green, and against that backdrop I made use of copious amounts of decomposed granite as ground cover and planted swaths of lavender. The overall effect was much simpler and paler, hazy, with light foliage and more silvery grays, which reiterated what was to be found within the house.

I staged the house in a simple and elegant style that did not detract from the flow, space and views we had painstakingly produced. And literally the first person who walked in and saw the rooms unfold effortlessly through to an exquisite exterior with expansive city views made an offer on the spot!

From the initial purchase and closing of escrow to the finished sale took only the six months that I had allocated to it. I had met all my goals for expense and delivery, and I was validated by the marketplace.

The experience with this project was to become the template for all my successes going forward—pour that champagne!

THE OUTSIDE

One of the first things we do is clear the grounds of overgrown foliage.

A simple but practical material to lay is concrete for steps.

Corbin has become a master fence builder on all our projects.

This is our go-to ground cover and it's eco-friendly!

You can't fail with borders of lavender and rosemary.

After realizing such a profit on my first solo renovation, I have to admit I was feeling a bit cocky.
Before escrow had even closed on the Hollywood
Hills home, I was already madly shopping for my
next project, scouring the online real estate sites,
which were just making themselves indispensable
to the marketplace, trying to find another house that
had staled on the market—a real white elephant.

I soon found one in the coveted valley neighborhood of Toluca Lake that had been sitting for 155 days despite its desirable location and the then overheated real estate market. I knew there had to be something really wrong with this property, and I was right—it was hideous!

Toluca Lake is an elegant Los Angeles neighborhood that surrounds a rare natural lake and the prestigious Lakeside Golf Club. Close to the Burbank Movie Studios, the area had attracted A-list Hollywood talent and became synonymous with movie star glamor of the '30s, '40s and '50s. Bob Hope, Bing Crosby and Frank Sinatra all resided there in between weekends in Palm Springs or Pebble Beach. And when Ronnie married Nancy, it was at the Toluca Lake home of his best friend and fellow screen idol William Holden.

Set behind oppressive dark gates, this house had an utterly charmless brick facade, and with a train wreck of an interior floor plan, dated awful finishes and an accumulation of bachelor-pad bad instincts, I would have my work cut out for me if I decided to go for this one.

Stepping inside, I noted the heaviness of the interior. The living and dining rooms were on either side of the foyer, which was lined floor to ceiling with mirror.

Past the living room was a truly horrible sunken rec room/man cave with all the requisite mishaps—wet bar, stained glass mirrors and a vomit green shag carpet to complete the look.

The kitchen and bathrooms made heavy use of bad laminated woods for cabinetry, complemented by age-stained walls and leaded windows.

In sum, this was not a house anyone would associate with Hollywood glamour. It was really the definition of a teardown.

But for me, it had great potential. It had width and room height to start with, and suddenly I could imagine both the interior and exterior with a change of palette. And with the smart black composite roof, I saw a clear vision of a painted brick Georgian scheme that was clean, spare and elegant.

My lowball offer was accepted, and with a budget agreed on with my contractor, I quickly set to work.

From what had been the living room, I created a beautiful and spacious kitchen, complete with its own fireplace.

Having stolen the original living room for a kitchen, I converted what had been the dining room into the new living room, and through a brilliant rehashing of awkward space, created a dining space off the kitchen. The flow of a home is one of the most important factors for reselling: it has to make sense.

I gained a bedroom and bathroom from the old kitchen site and reconfigured the master into a larger, lighter suite by adding, where possible, windows and French doors that opened onto the garden—another very important resell ingredient.

There were a couple of budget setbacks, like discovering the HVAC system needed replacing, but as I was learning, sometimes having less to spend can influence creativity!

I did, however, splurge on two upgrades that I considered to be the wow factors of this project: the kitchen island countertop and the light that was to hang suspended over it.

When the primary construction was completed and all surfaces were raw and ready to be claimed, I set to work on what became the biggest transformation of all: the palette change.

I had decided on that first day that a clean, crisp, bright white would change the whole dynamic of this house, and it did. Top to toe in white, with a sage gray accent on the windows and doors, created a seamless and expansive feel.

The variations on a theme of white establish an excellent neutral palette upon which to build any number of overlaying color stories. White is a springboard for those who want to play with bold color or those who want to double down with neutral tones. Either way, a white background is an inviting burst of gesso. I love white and find in it almost infinite varieties and tonal differentiations based on underlying materials, time of day, and surrounding complementary hues.

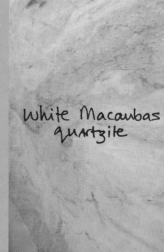

Decorator's white by Benjamin Moore

Subway tile with gray grout

Concrete effect Floor tile

White Macaubas quartzite

Some of the best-kept secrets in LA are the countless suppliers of stone, marble, granite and tile, and I always go deep into the San Fernando Valley for my finds.

My decision to cover the entire fireplace wall with white subway tile and gray grout made a dramatically graphic statement.

The master bath got a cool floor made from Moroccan cement tiles I had left over from a previous job. This allowed me the extravagant lighting purchases.

I now have to admit that this lovely Georgian home was really an eye-opener, as I was fast staging it for sale, and as in the previous home, I purposely scaled back the drama and vitality of the furnishings so as not to detract from my exercise in tonal restraint.

The resulting subdued elegance worked well to showcase the spare and tranquil effect that white and neutral shading can provide.

I listed the house and in came the offers.

UNIFYING THE SPACE

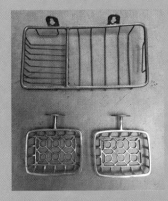

On our travels we came across these beautiful vintage soap dishes which we used in the bathrooms.

I mixed brass throughout the house by using these cabinet pulls in both kitchen and bathrooms.

I try to find a unique countertop that will work in both kitchen and bathrooms.

My signature gray floor stain helps unify the whole house.

Saving money doesn't always mean compromising on style. The cabinet pulls are from Home Depot and the faucet from build.com.

Simplicity

Sherman Oaks

After a long and happy run in Studio City, we backed into a another paradigm shift that would have truly lasting consequences: the would-be buyers were so enamored with our thoroughly family-honed lifestyle that they wanted to buy the home plus furnishings—lock, stock and barrel. As all the boys were on the move, Corbin and I decided we could happily roll with that proposition for the second time in our lives. (Remember, we had pulled a similar gypsy-like maneuver when we cashed out our Beverly Hills home.) Although we had loved finding, fixing and furnishing the place, most of the pieces now belonged where we had placed them.

Underneath the realization to let go was the very real desire to once again lighten our load and prepare to become empty nesters. It was hard to part with the refectory table that had been the touchstone for a whole chapter of domestic bliss, but I knew from experience that there were fascinating pieces of furniture waiting to be found that would complement our next habitat perfectly. For Corbin and me, the hunt was always the fun part anyway, and we decided our future moves would be all about simplification and refinement.

By a stroke of serendipitous good luck, we found ourselves looking at a midcentury modern beauty that had fallen out of escrow and was waiting for us to arrive! We were meant to have looked at it months before, but I could not find the address so decided to pass on the viewing, which subsequently enabled us to get the house for a deal, as is very often the case in this situation.

Corbin and I loved this simple '50s post and beam the minute we saw it. It would be the perfect pit stop for everything we needed and wanted to accomplish in the next year and allow us to reflect for a while, take a much-needed reprieve. In a very Zen way—no big brainstorming necessary—the ultimate scheme for the renovation revealed itself to us both on that first visit. The house was dated, but as a vessel it was perfectly intact, a sixty-year-old template for unencumbered living that was perfect for a family in transition.

The expansively easy vibe was already there: the layout and the glass and the soaring rectangular geometries all served to effortlessly collaborate with the laid-back lifestyles that would play out within and not impede them with the formality of a floor plan.

There was work to be done, but nothing too aggressive or complicated. As it turned out, there were no real headaches or pitfalls on this project.

From inception through renovation, the walls of glass and ceiling heights allowed by post and beam construction were a daily inspiration. Not to mention, they framed spectacular valley views under a canopy of a sprawling old-growth California oak.

The indoor/outdoor paradigm informed much of what we did at that house. The mid-century aesthetic was already foundationally established; we just piggybacked on top of that and enjoyed the free ride. I felt light and free, creative and energized by the constant contact with the natural world.

With regard to the various extensive surfaces—horizontal and vertical planes that really defined the interior space—I found the original hardwood parquet floors to be in great shape and had them sanded and, yes, stained gray. In the kitchen, office space and bathrooms I had a new screed of concrete laid, which we matte sealed. We were lucky the original steel-cased sliders were in great shape, and all we had to add were any new steel single and double casement windows to various rooms for added light.

We were also able to reuse all of the kitchen lower cabinets—which we painted a muddy blue-gray—together with their hardware. This coupled with new Caesarstone Fresh Concrete countertops, bright white painted brick walls and sparkling new steel appliances really turned this inspired treasure into an upgraded jewel.

We really didn't touch the floor plan except to delicately remove a few interior walls and open the space to extend the view even further within the house. We opened the kitchen to living areas, creating a version of our now signature hub—and massaged three bedrooms, three baths and a powder room out of the original two bedrooms and one bath, which, although they were on a smaller scale, worked perfectly within the new flow we were creating.

All of our experience and proficiencies came together in Sherman Oaks. We harmonized all of the elements we had discovered and honed over twenty-eight years of renovating—from our beloved white walls of tile and skim coats of concrete on kitchen and bathroom floors, to the light stains we found so beautiful on resurrected hardwood flooring, to easily sourcing midcentury-style furnishings locally, to using an appropriate and soothing color palette that was light, white and bright.

We hand-picked this slab of walnut and had a local artisan make a coffee table out of it.

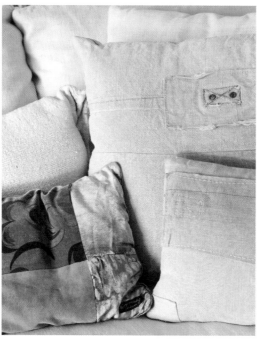

The sourcing of furnishings proceeded in this Zen-inspired midcentury aesthetic: the dining table and chairs from Organic Modernism and other vintage pieces from MidcenturyLA.

Color was added through the ongoing encampment of books, pillows, throws and accessories that were cycled through this house, cherished possessions and artworks that we've trundled around with us from the very beginning.

After we sold Studio City and virtually everything in it, we were able to make the move to our Zen retreat in Sherman Oaks with nothing more than could fit into a drive off POD. Sherman Oaks was a lesson in downsizing and simplifying while still living colorfully within the bare bones of a structure—a huge achievement compared to previous moves.

We had accomplished everything we set out to do, negotiating our family into its next chapter, learning to live with less, calmly exploring our future prospects while we quietly contemplated the path that got us to this unobstructed view of valley lights and our own horizon.

SIMPLE SOLUTIONS

To add interest to all of the interior doors, I painted a gray base.

This may be an odd pair, but I picked them up for five bucks at an old plumbing store in the valley.

Corbin designed and built these open pullout drawers in the kitchen for easy access.

I had saved a couple of my favorite brass hooks from Spain to be used in this house too.

Comfort

Mas Maroc, France

One day recently, Corbin and I worked out the math of our nomadic marriage and were startled to realize that during our nearly thirty years together we've already lived in twenty different houses. Wow! But despite our itinerant lifestyle, an ongoing parallel dream of mine to eventually settle into one single place that we could rely on emotionally for the rest of our lives ran in the background of my mind. I wanted a place where our truly prized possessions could finally come to rest and form a cushiony clubhouse for all of us to recharge from wherever else we happened to be.

I wanted at long last a "forever" home, specifically, a farmhouse property in the sunny South of France. Don't think gentle lavender fields of Provence or the glittering coastline of the Alps-Martimes. The region of my dreams was the rugged agricultural country that hugs the border with Spain—sparsely populated with stone buildings, rocky soil, and an arid climate.

My mother had been living there for decades, and both of my sisters had moved nearby, so I was desperate to find a place near my family for the LA branch of the clan. However, original farmhouses were hard to come by.

Two years and a couple of near misses later, I came across a rather ugly but humble-looking pink stucco farmhouse while scanning the Internet. I immediately sent my sister Lucy to check it out, and she told me to get on a plane that night! I opened escrow on it forty-eight hours later.

The location was ideal—five minutes from my mother and just ten from the sparkling Mediterranean—a huge selling point. The house itself was very rustic, a practical shelter for local farm laborers. The terra-cotta tile roof was in excellent condition, but the interior was dark and closed in, with low ceilings and crumbling plaster walls. Its saving grace was the beautiful stone I uncovered, buried beneath that pink stucco. My instincts had been right: this house was 400 years old.

We hired a local "no English spoken" contractor, Jean-François, to handle any regulatory constraints we would encounter; He also understood the simple, artisanal aesthetic we wanted to preserve in every aspect of this remodel while creating a four-bedroom, three-bathroom configuration from a relatively small space.

We also wanted to gain more light but were informed that on the back side of the house the reason there were only two very thin slit windows was for protection from the ever-present Tramontane wind that howled off the Pyrenees behind us, bringing sand and debris with it.

Although I appreciated this very practical link to history, I decided that light was more important, and so forged ahead with the addition of as many French doors and windows as I was legally allowed.

A modern master bath was created by expanding outward onto an existing balcony, and an ill-used mezzanine area was transformed into a bedroom loft for two.

As the gentle sandblasting of the stucco revealed the smooth fieldstone walls outside, the installation of new windows and disentanglement of rooms inside gave life to an open, light environment that began to take on a real Mediterranean feel.

Jean-Francois proved to be indispensable, and he even managed to carve out a fourth bedroom/bathroom downstairs from the outside lean-to shed.

Downstairs, I applied my tried and tested "great room" layout technique, opening up the entire floor from wall to wall. And after the whitewashing of all surfaces, the painting of all floors, my Greek-inspired farmhouse was ready to go!

I had a lot of fun sourcing product in a foreign country, such as the beautiful aged marble sinks and antique tile from Spain. I even repurposed a brass faucet my mother was throwing out for use in our bathroom.

Most of the basics, like the kitchen appliances and plumbing fixtures, I found at the local Leroy Merlin, France's answer to Home Depot.

We built a concrete
seat to the right of the
fireplace to gain more
room for our family
of six.

DON McCULLIN

During this French renovation, we were also busy downsizing stateside for our move to Sherman Oaks, and were deep in the process of "getting rid of stuff!" But when comparing the cost of buying new for France or shipping there what we already owned in LA, we were happy to discover it would be far cheaper to ship it! So off went a twenty-foot container—door to door—with the comfortable, familiar pieces to furnish our family farmhouse.

Everything from bedframes made by Corbin, to sofas, linens, books, artwork and even kitchen utensils were in that container. We did not have to buy a thing for France. (Well, maybe the odd tea towel.)

This is where we gather for an impromptu glass of wine when the wind kicks up outside.

Outside, we simply landscaped areas that blended into the surrounding fields of vines and were hardy enough to withstand the elements. Cypress, olives, fig, pine and our favorite lavender were planted throughout.

We put in a family-size pool, surrounded by concrete decking and ample al fresco BBQ area—for the all important summer gatherings.

Collioure is our local seaside village, famous for its gathering of the Impressionist artists.

Now we travel to France every summer and fully embrace the regional culture. Mornings, we swim in the Mediterranean, grab a coffee and head to the local farmers market. We live on fish—sardines, moules, calamar—which are available in abundance and are the mainstay of Catalan cuisine. Plus local cheeses made from the milk of the mountain goats that we see all over the landscape.

We relish the uninterrupted time we're able to share with our family and friends.

We find comfort in the familiarity of our own lifestyle, taking comfort in the fresh air, letting go of "things," which require so much maintenance and care.

My dream of an easy, comfortable family retreat—a place where we could all kick back and put our feet up—was finally and totally realized. In a way, what began as a dream, ended as one.

BACK TO BASICS

We find vintage linens at the local vides-greniers and brocantes.

Even our terrier mix, Rosie, loves my gray floors.

I ordered these cool, simple sconces online from a German company.

These chunky vintage horse-tack hooks can take the weight of the whole family.

We showed Jean-François how to make our signature toilet roll holders.

A QUICK RECAP

- First we look for the space we can open to create that "hub" of the house. This will become the kitchen/living space.

- We always choose a house with a garden and a couple of mature trees that we can work with. They create shade and atmosphere and give the property weight and a sense of history.

- We usually clear the grounds of old shrubbery and add DG, lavender, succulents and olives to give it a sophisticated European feel.

- We always look for original features and architecture that can be salvaged and upgraded. We care about keeping the integrity of a home. We have never razed a house to the ground. Part of the fun is tackling the challenges an old house gives us.

- We add windows and French doors to flood the house with light.

- We stick with the neutral whites in both paint and tile, which allows the texture to be added in art and furnishings.

- We have discovered the beauty in gray-staining wood floors; this has become a signature statement for us.

- Unity is very important when we are choosing materials, colors, fixtures, fittings, hardware and lighting. "Less is more" is our motto here. We usually run with three or four complementary tones for both inside and out: the wall/ceiling color, the woodwork color, the floor color and perhaps one more accent color. We use these throughout.

- The same with hardware. We choose door, faucet and lighting hardware together so it all flows. This may be a mix of two metals, but we balance the use throughout. We also throw in a few hooks and a soap dish or two that we have collected from our travels. They make the house unique and bring a story to the process.

- We always work within a budget and start by saving as many original parts as we can during the demolition phase. This is very often lighting and hardware, which I collect for later use. I will then build my new hardware and color scheme off these originals if they are worth using.

- We budget by buying appliances during sales—it's always fun to get a deal!

- We learn how to adapt and compromise within our budget, and if we overspend on the bathroom tile, then we have to cut back on the price of the oven. I find that tightening the belt brings out creativity. If I cannot afford a tile backsplash behind the bathroom sinks then I will paint a wide border of gloss paint as the backsplash. It never fails!

IN CLOSING

by Corbin Bernsen

When we first had the idea for this book, both Amanda and I started from the simple place of wanting to share some of our design process and show some examples of the finished products. Along the way, we knew we would have to incorporate our family homes—I mean, we've lived in most of the houses we've designed and flipped, so it became natural to include our more personal story in these pages. What we didn't expect was to find ourselves with such a vivid picture of our history, and how creating these homes, and very specifically, the spaces within, would become a significant imprint that so perfectly summarized our family and lives together.

I was certain that the duty of "final thoughts" would fall upon me—after all, I wrote the opening remarks! I hesitated to tackle it, however, in advance of actually seeing the final book—or at least its rough form. I wanted to experience the book as the reader (those who actually read the words) or viewer (those who flip through and just look at the pictures) might. So I waited. When I finally sat down to take a look, I committed to studying it cover to cover in one go and to do my best to remove myself from the story, experience it with fresh eyes. I was astonished, to say the least. Not because it was the best book I've ever read or the pictures were so awesome—which I think they are——but rather seeing so strongly, in hard evidence, that my life—our lives have been truly blessed.

I've long held that family is the cornerstone, the foundation upon which all else is built, including the home. I've questioned over the years the practicality and sensibility of moving so many times, never having that "family home" that one lives in for years and years. And while I've seen great examples of how that works so wonderfully with friends and other families, our way has also worked, and in fact not only enhanced our family life but also defined it. We've been nomads, living day by day and being sheltered tent by tent. And I firmly believe the one thing that has truly made that possible is the spaces we've created in each of our homes, and our lives, that allow for light—that kind of migration birds enjoy: "open skies," if you will—limitless, living season to season. And with that space comes an inherent willingness to always have the door to our home open—an Open House—for us to come and go freely and invite others in to share the wonders of it all.

RESOURCES

LIGHTING:

cedarandmoss.com
Beautiful modern and mid-century inspired lighting.

shoponefortythree.com
Budget lighting and accessories.

schoolhouse.com
US manufacturers of lighting and classic goods.

visualcomfort.com
Large lighting site where you can shop all designers.

badiadesign.com
Moroccan lighting and furnishings.

practicalprops.com
Specializes in new, vintage and reproduction lighting.

PLUMBING:

signaturehardware.com
Nice selection of reasonably priced bath and kitchen supplies.

squaredealplumbing.com
Hard-to-find vintage plumbing fixtures and reglazing.

Build.com
Budget plumbing fixtures.

agaliving.com
Traditional British ovens and cooking accessories.

BUILDING MATERIALS:

prime building materials
818.503.4242
If you know what you want, the best place for flagstones.

Stoneville.com
A place you can handpick your own slab of quartz, granite or marble.

osh.com
For paint, dropcloths and hardware.

homedepot.com
For basic white tile, hardware and wood for fencing.

HDsupply.com
For doors and windows on a budget.

PLANTING:

Vineland Nursery
818.505.8218
Reasonably priced plants and small trees.

FURNITURE AND ACCESSORIES:

The Pasadena Rose Bowl Flea Market
#1 on our list for the best place to shop in LA, second Sunday of every month.

Big Daddy's Antiques
BDAntiques.com
Antique and reproduction furniture and accessories.

Olde Good Things
Ogtstore.com
Reclaimed building materials and architectural artifacts.

MidcenturyLA.com
Imported midcentury furniture from Denmark and Sweden.

Organicmodernism.com
Midcentury-inspired new furniture with a twist.

Roomandboard.com
Nice selection of modern furniture and accessories made in the USA.

HDButtercup.com
Great furniture sales.

abchome.com
When in New York, it's a must.

Lostandfoundshop.com
A beautifully curated home goods store.

Pasadenaville.com
Hand-crafted tables from live-edge wood slabs.

FABRICS:

Kathrynireland.com
Beautiful collection of fabrics.

Georgesmith.com
Fabric and furniture makers.

Bennisonfabrics.com
Beautiful British fabrics.

Ianmankin.com
Classic contemporary fabrics.

Anta.co.uk
Fabrics and accessories made
in Scotland.

RESOURCES IN EUROPE:

L'isle-sur-la-Sorgue, France,
Antiques market.

Souks in Marrakesh, Morocco
Rugs, accessories.

Drummonds-uk.com
Specializing in bathrooms.

Judy Greenwood Antiques
657 Fulham Rd, London SW6
020.7736.6037.
Funky antiques and objects.

Rupertspira.com
Beautiful ceramics.

labourandwait.co.uk
Carefully selected home wares.

Ultima Parada
La Bisbal, Spain
Vintage shop and restaurant.
Eclectic mix of furniture and
objects, worth a visit.

A BIG THANK-YOU

To my son Oliver for understanding my vision and taking the lead in the design, art direction and editing of this book.

To Mel Bordeaux for helping me focus and get the words on paper.

To Kathryn Ireland for introducing me to Madge Baird and Gibbs Smith, and to Madge for saying "Yes."

To all the photographers that have captured our homes so beautifully.

To all our friends and family here who share in these memories, and to my family in France, who greet us enthusiastically every summer with a bounty of food and wine!

To my other boys, Henry, Angus and Finley, and dogs Digby and Rosie, who make the family complete.

And lastly, to my husband, Corbin, for his unconditional love and support through all these crazy moves and for his eloquent words.

PHOTO CREDITS

21 20 19 18 17   5 4 3 2

Text © 2017 Amanda Pays and Corbin Bernsen

Photograph credits on page 174

Published by
Gibbs Smith
P.O. Box 667
Layton, Utah 84041

1.800.835.4993 orders

www.gibbs-smith.com

Designed by Oliver Bernsen

Gibbs Smith books are printed on paper produced from sustainable PEFC-certified forest/controlled wood source. Learn more at www.pefc.org.

Printed and bound in Hong Kong

Library of Congress Control Number: 2017935134

ISBN: 978-1-4236-4735-5

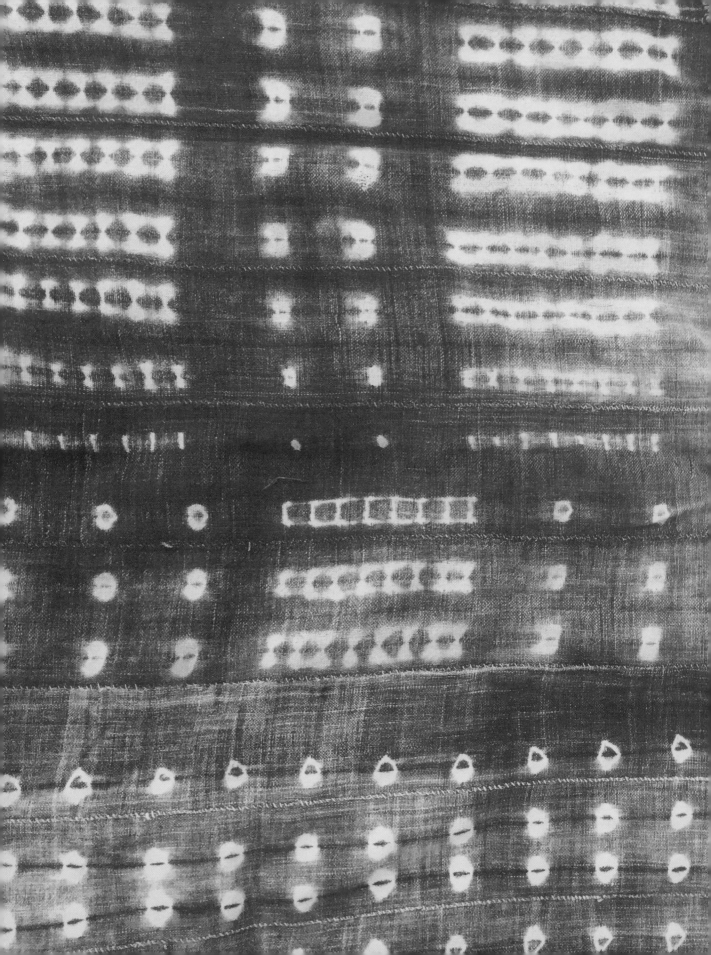